MW00904939

BONUS

Want a Bonus?

Download The Vision Board Freebie:
5 Steps to Create a Vision Board that Works E-Book
&
Vision Board Goal Setting Workbook
Link: bit.ly/vision_board_freebie

60 Positive Affirmation cards + 30 Inspirational quote cards For Vision Boards

I AM CAPABLE AND I AM STRONG.

YOU LEARN MORE FROM FAILURE THAN SUCCESS. DON'T LET IT STOP YOU. FAILURE BUILDS CHARACTER

IF I WANT SOMETHING BADLY ENOUGH, I CAN FIND A WAY TO MAKE IT HAPPEN.

I AM BRAVE, RESILIENT AND STRONG.

THE FUTURE MAY BE UNCERTAIN BUT THAT WON'T STOP ME LOOKING FORWARD WITH HOPE.

ONLY SURROUND YOURSELF WITH PEOPLE WHO WILL LIFT YOU HIGHER

60 Positive Affirmation cards + 30 Inspirational quote cards For Your Vision Board

⬇ DOWNLOAD

Link: bit.ly/affirmations-quotes-cards

Or Use QR Code

Instagram QR Code

FOLLOW US

Follow Us On Instagram: @manifesthappinesschannel
Follow us on Amazon: amazon.com/author/mh-press
Our Website and Blog: manifest-happiness.com
Our Printables Shop: shop.manifest-happiness.com
Subscribe to Our Youtube Channel:
youtube.com/c/manifesthappinesschannel

MANIFESTHAPPINESSCHANNEL

Check out our 2025 vision board clip art book on Amazon

(ASIN : B0DDJBX9VG)

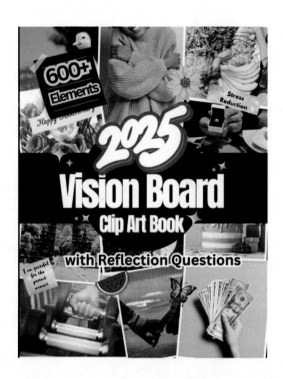

link : bit.ly/2025-vision-board-book

Or use QR Code

Calm

Relaxation

Peace

Gratitude

love

BREATHE

ZEN

COMFORT

Mindfulness

BALANCE

unwind

SERENITY

MEDITATE

COZY

FREE

SAFE

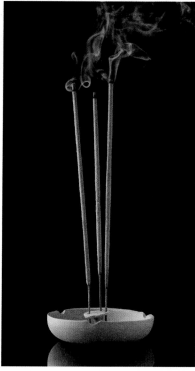
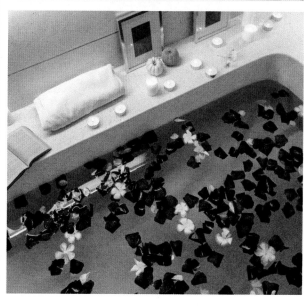

I am calm and in control

I release all tension from my mind and body

I am worthy of rest and relaxation

I inhale peace and exhale stress

I am surrounded by calming energy

My mind is at ease, my soul is at peace

Every breath I take fills me with calm

I let go of what I cannot change and embrace serenity

"You can't always control what goes on outside, but you can always control what goes on inside."
Wayne Dyer

"Relax. Yu are enough. You have enough. You do enough."
Unknown

"Almost everything will work again if you unplug it for a few minutes, including you."
Anne Lamott

"Stress is caused by being 'here' but wanting to be 'there'."
Eckhart Tolle

"The greatest weapon against stress is our ability to choose one thought over another."
William James

"Don't anticipate trouble or worry about what may never happen. Keep in the sunlight."
Benjamin Franklin

"Take rest; a field that has rested gives a bountiful crop."
Ovid

"Within you, there is a stillness and a sanctuary to which you can retreat at any time and be yourself."
Hermann Hesse

REST & RELAXATION

relax

RELAX

it's TIME -TO- Relax

it's TIME -TO- Relax

Relax

RELAX and CHILL

Keep Calm

cozy vibes

CALM DOWN

COZY -AND- COMFY

Made in the USA
Las Vegas, NV
03 December 2024

13275397R00024